COMPUTER GRAPHICS

FROM CONCEPT TO CONSUMER

BY KEVIN CUNNINGHAM

CHILDREN'S PRESS®

An Imprint of Scholastic Inc.
New York Toronto London Auckland Sydney
Mexico City New Delhi Hong Kong
Danbury, Connecticut

CONTENT CONSULTANT
Dr. John C. Hart, Professor of Computer Science, University of Illinois at Urbana-Champaign

PHOTOGRAPHS © 2014: Alamy Images: 3, 5 left, 26 right, 27, 36 bottom, 37, 43
(AF archive), 23 (David R. Frazier Photolibrary, Inc.), 24 (epa european pressphoto agency
b.v.), 26 left, 50 (Moviestore collection Ltd.), 42 (PhotoAlto), 52 (Pictorial Press Ltd.), 51
(United Archives GmbH); AP Images: 15 (Bob Galbraith), 58 (Frank Franklin II), 10 (The
Inamori Foundation), 14; Boeing Images/William Fetter: 9; Corbis Images/Michael Macor/
San Francisco Chronicle: 11; Courtesy of Diana Sear: 40; Everett Collection: 18, 19 bottom
(20th Century Fox), 16 (Buena Vista), 55 bottom (Focus Features), 55 top (Lucasfilm Ltd.),
54 (Mary Evans/MGM/Ronald Grant), 56 (Mary Evans/New Line Cinema/Wingnut Films/
Lord Dritte Productions DE/Ronald Grant), 5 right, 28, 44, 47, 48, 53 (New Line), 39, 41
(Paramount Pictures), 46 (Rankin-Bass Productions), 29, 49, 57 (Warner Brothers), 4 left, 4
right, 19 top, 25, 30 left, 30 right, 31, 38; Getty Images: 35 (AFP), 22 (Greg Pease), cover
(Paper Boat Creative): 17; Media Bakery: 6, 13, 59; Shutterstock, Inc.: 8 (Lisa F. Young), 20
(wavebreakmedia); The Image Works: 32 (Disney/Pixar/TopFoto), 36 top (National News/
Topham), 12 (SSPL), 34 (Syracuse Newspapers/D Blume).

LIBRARY OF CONGRESS CATALOGING-IN-PUBLICATION DATA
Cunningham, Kevin, 1966–
  Computer graphics : from concept to consumer / by Kevin Cunningham.
    p. cm. — (Calling all innovators: A Career for You)
  Includes bibliographical references and index.
  ISBN 978-0-531-26520-8 (lib. bdg.) — ISBN 978-0-531-22008-5 (pbk.)
1. Computer graphics — History — Juvenile literature. 2. Computer graphics — Vocational
guidance — Juvenile literature. I. Title.
  T385.C8535 2013
  006.6023 — dc23   2012034206

Science, technology, engineering, arts, and math are the fields that drive innovation. Whether they are finding ways to make our lives easier or developing the latest entertainment, the people who work in these fields are changing the world for the better. Do you have what it takes to join the ranks of today's greatest innovators? Read on to discover whether computer graphics are a career for you.

TABLE *of* CONTENTS

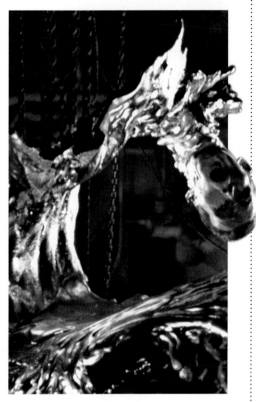

Terminator 2: Judgment Day *won an Academy Award for Visual Effects in 1992.*

Avatar *is the highest grossing movie of all time.*

Tron: Legacy *is the sequel to the 1982 sci-fi classic* Tron.

Actor Andy Serkis wore a motion capture suit for his role as Gollum in the Lord of the Rings *movies.*

People in the United States and Canada spend around $10 billion on movie tickets each year.

CHAPTER ONE

SEEING THE FUTURE

As you walk into the theater carrying your bucket of hot popcorn, you search for the best open seat. You and your friends settle down in a row near the front and look up at the enormous screen just as the lights dim. After some previews for upcoming movies, the opening scene begins to unfold before you. On-screen, a massive alien spaceship lands in New York City. As the evil aliens launch their attack, a team of costumed heroes arrives on the scene. Huge explosions shake the theater as the characters do battle. The heroes fly through the sky, dodging beams of colorful energy launched by the alien weapons. They effortlessly pick up cars and buses to throw at the aliens and hold up damaged buildings to keep them from falling. You know that none of these things could actually happen. But how did the filmmakers make these incredible scenes look so real?

SUPERB SOFTWARE

1961	early 1980s	1986	1990
Sketchpad is created.	Reyes rendering changes animation.	RenderMan is used for first Pixar film.	Photoshop 1.0 is released.

THE IMPOSSIBLE COMES TO LIFE

Computer graphics allow artists and animators to create anything they can imagine, from a carefully recreated historical event to the vast landscape of an imaginary alien planet. They can build entire worlds from the ground up and fill them with characters. They can also alter footage of real-life scenes to make it look as if impossible things are happening. They do this by using computer software to draw and animate 3D models of their creations.

Today, you see computer graphics everywhere. They are a major part of video games and modern movies. They are so present in our lives today that it is hard to believe they have only existed since the 1960s!

Around 56 percent of all homes in the United States have at least one modern video game system.

Once considered toys for kids, video games have in recent years become popular with people of all ages.

WIRELESS GAME
CONTROLLERS

THE BEGINNING

In 1961, Ivan Sutherland, a student at the Massachusetts Institute of Technology (MIT), created an early computer art program called Sketchpad. Using Sketchpad, an artist could draw images directly on a computer screen using a device called a light pen. When the tip of the pen was placed against the monitor, it interacted with the screen and allowed the user to draw simple shapes.

William Fetter, an artist and designer for the Boeing aircraft company, used Sketchpad when designing aircraft. He coined the term *computer graphics* in the early 1960s. In 1964, Fetter used Sketchpad to draw a wireframe model of a person around which he would design aircraft cockpits. This model, called Boeing Man, was the first computer model of a human being ever created.

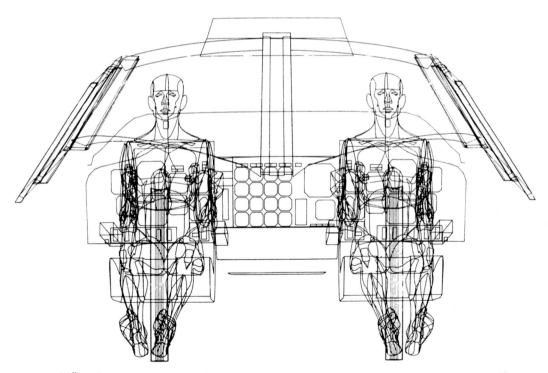

William Fetter's Boeing Man model was used to show how humans would fit into airplane cockpit designs.

FANTASTIC FIRSTS

Computer graphics advanced quickly as creative minds began to find new uses for them. In 1962, Sutherland's fellow MIT student Steve Russell led a team in creating *Spacewar!*, one of the earliest video games. In the game, two players controlled spaceships that moved through a field of stars shooting missiles at each other. The graphics were made up of no more than bright green lines and dots on a black background. Despite this simple appearance, *Spacewar!* became the first widely popular video game.

The same year *Spacewar!* was launched, scientist E. E. Zajac made the first computer-generated animated film. It was a demonstration to show how a new type of satellite technology worked. While the film's animation may not seem as thrilling as a modern computer-animated blockbuster movie, it broke new ground in the possibilities for computer graphics.

In 2012, Ivan Sutherland won Japan's Kyoto Prize for his lifetime contributions to computer graphics technology.

Edwin Catmull became president of the Walt Disney Company and Pixar Animation Studios, which has created many of the most popular computer-animated movies.

NEW WAYS TO DRAW

In 1968, Ivan Sutherland became a professor at the University of Utah, where he established a graphics laboratory that would produce many of the industry's most important innovators.

Two members of Sutherland's Utah team, Henri Gouraud and Bui Tuong Phong, invented

EDWIN CATMULL

One of Ivan Sutherland's students, Edwin Catmull, developed groundbreaking animation software. Catmull created one program that allowed animators to cover computer-generated surfaces with **textures**. Another allowed computers to **render** curved surfaces. One of Catmull's most famous early creations was a 3D animation of his hand. The animation was later used in the 1976 science fiction film *Futureworld*. It was the first use of 3D computer animation in a Hollywood movie.

new techniques for **shading** digital images. Their work resulted in 3D models with smooth, continuous surfaces.

FIRST THINGS FIRST

GETTING PERSONAL

Today, there are computers almost everywhere you look. Even the smartphones and tablets that many people carry everyday are powerful enough to create and display detailed graphics. But prior to the rise in popularity of personal computers (PCs) in the 1970s, computer systems were generally found only at universities, government facilities, or large companies. They were massive, highly expensive systems that often took up entire rooms and were comparatively limited in their abilities. PCs changed everything by shrinking computer systems down to a more manageable size and price. By the 1980s, millions of people around the world had PCs in their homes and offices. As the use of PCs became more widespread, so did computer graphics software. Today, anyone with a creative idea can produce high quality computer graphics as long as they have access to a computer.

INCREDIBLE INTERFACES

Today, we are accustomed to using mice, keyboards, and touch screens to click and drag colorful **icons** and windows around our computer desktops. However, early PC operating systems were controlled almost entirely by text commands. Users could type commands into the computer or select items from numbered menus. It wasn't until the late 1970s that researchers at Xerox and Apple began planning graphical user **interfaces**, or GUIs, for PCs. These early GUIs introduced the graphical "desktop" still used in most of today's operating systems. As graphics became a major part of using PCs, computer graphics software became more and more common. Today, Microsoft's Windows and Apple's OS X and iOS are some of the most popular GUIs.

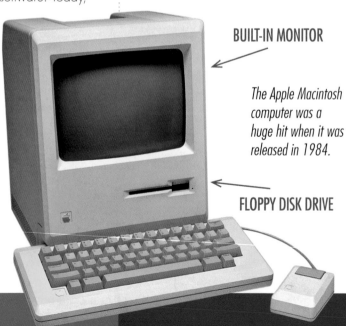

BUILT-IN MONITOR

The Apple Macintosh computer was a huge hit when it was released in 1984.

FLOPPY DISK DRIVE

Even everyday home and school computers can be used to create computer graphics.

PAINTING ON SCREEN

One of the very first computer graphics programs was SuperPaint, created by Xerox's Richard Shoup and Alvy Ray Smith in the early 1970s. It allowed users to create artwork using **virtual** paintbrushes and custom shapes and lines, and enabled users to fill images with color. NASA used SuperPaint to create animations to explain a 1978 space mission.

MacPaint was a graphics painting program that came packaged with the first Apple Macintosh computer when it was released in 1984. Like SuperPaint, it allowed users to create graphics using shapes and drawing tools. Millions of people purchased Macintosh computers, and many of these people quickly began using MacPaint to create simple graphics.

ADOBE'S ADVANCEMENTS

As technology improved and PC users became more accustomed to creating computer graphics, a demand grew for more powerful graphics software. A company called Adobe Systems founded by John Warnock and Charles Geschke, soon released software that would change computer graphics forever.

Illustrator, first released in 1987, offered users advanced tools for creating vector graphics, which are commonly used to create typefaces and logos. Photoshop, released three years later, provided a powerful system for editing digital photographs. Today, updated versions of both programs remain important tools for casual users and computer graphics professionals alike. ✺

BRINGING IT HOME

After the success of early creations such as *Spacewar!*, video games only grew in popularity. Game makers began competing to create more interesting graphics. Throughout the 1970s, a wide variety of new games were released for home consoles, arcade machines, and PCs. At first, early games such as *Pong* used simple, one-color graphics, just as *Spacewar!* had. By the end of the decade, though, arcade games such as *Space Invaders* were dazzling players with colorful, more complex graphics. With the release of the Nintendo Entertainment System in 1985, video games became more popular than ever. Millions of people around the world could enjoy cutting-edge graphics right in their living rooms.

Atari sold more than 30 million units of its Video Computer System, helping to popularize home video games.

PAC-MAN HAS REMAINED POPULAR SINCE ITS INTRODUCTION IN 1980.

KNOBS FOR CHANGING CHANNELS AND ADJUSTING VOLUME

CONTROLLERS ATTACHED TO CONSOLE USING CORDS

Filmmaker George Lucas was an early adopter of computer graphics technology. In 1997, he took advantage of recent computer graphics advances to enhance his original Star Wars *movies of the 1970s and 1980s.*

REALISTIC RENDERING

In 1979, *Star Wars* creator George Lucas established a computer graphics group within his Lucasfilm production company. Lucas hired graphics innovator Ed Catmull to lead the group. Other graphics experts, including SuperPaint co-creator Alvy Ray Smith, also joined. The group specialized in creating special effects for films and researching new graphics technology.

One of the group's most important early creations was a graphics system called Reyes (short for "Renders Everything You Ever Saw"). It allowed computers to render **photorealistic** 3D graphics.

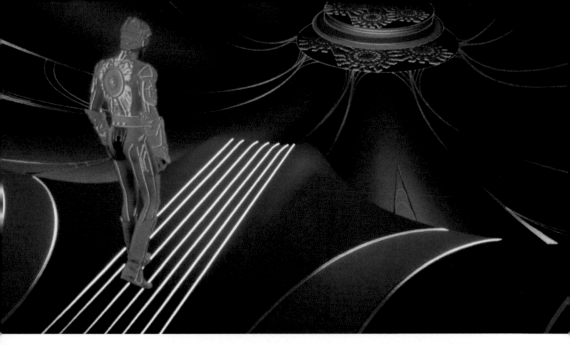

Tron's creators used a blend of computer graphics, live-action footage, and hand-drawn animation to bring the movie's virtual world to life.

AT THE MOVIES

The 1982 Disney film *Tron* tells the story of a computer programmer who becomes trapped inside a virtual world. It wowed audiences by featuring more than 15 minutes of computer-generated animation. As computer-generated vehicles sped across futuristic computer-generated landscapes, moviegoers couldn't believe their eyes. They had never seen anything like it.

The graphics engineers on the *Tron* project faced major hurdles. For one thing, they had to invent much of the graphics technology themselves. Another problem was that the computers of the time were not powerful enough to render as much detail as the filmmakers wanted in the graphics. Even with these difficulties, however, the film kicked off a widespread interest in using computer graphics in movies.

"Without *Tron*, there would be no *Toy Story*."
—Pixar's John Lasseter

THE BIRTH OF PIXAR

In 1986, George Lucas decided to sell the Lucasfilm computer graphics group. Apple founder Steve Jobs purchased the group and provided money to turn it into a new company, which he called Pixar. At first, Pixar focused on creating computer graphics hardware. That all changed with *Luxo Jr.*, a two-minute animated film featuring two desk lamps playing with a ball.

Pixar's John Lasseter, a former Disney animator, used Pixar's technology to create titled *Luxo Jr.* Jobs was impressed with Lasseter's work and encouraged the company to continue creating new animated films. By the early 1990s, Pixar had given up its hardware business to focus on animation.

Pixar's animators used a software system called RenderMan to create their films. RenderMan was based on Reyes rendering. It allowed the animators to create computer-generated shadows for the first time in movie history.

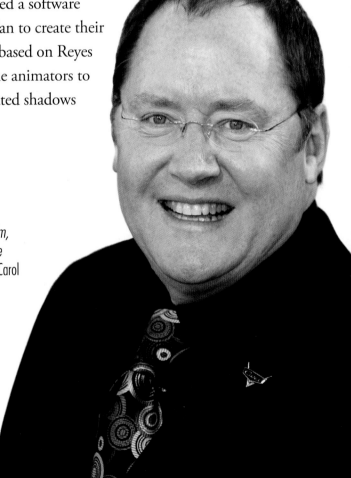

Before going to work for Lucasfilm, John Lasseter helped animate the Disney films Mickey's Christmas Carol *and* The Fox and the Hound.

The computer-generated pseudopod was one of the highlights of 1989's The Abyss.

BIG SCREEN BLOCKBUSTERS

While movies such as *Tron* and the *Star Wars* trilogy pioneered the use of computer graphics in movies, some of the biggest advancements in the technology came in later years. During the 1980s and 1990s, filmmakers such as James Cameron and Steven Spielberg used computer graphics to help create some of the biggest blockbusters of all time.

THE ABYSS

In 1989, George Lucas's visual effects company, Industrial Light & Magic (ILM), created a computer-generated sea creature for James Cameron's *The Abyss*. James Cameron had asked ILM to create a "pseudopod" made of water. It had to move smoothly, change shape, and do something almost unheard of for a computer-generated image: interact with the human actors.

It took ILM eight months to create the scenes with the pseudopod. For all that work, the creature appeared on-screen for just under 75 seconds. ILM used several shots of actor Ed Harris to recreate Harris's face on the pseudopod. *The Abyss* was not a hit. But the pseudopod remains a landmark in computer graphics history.

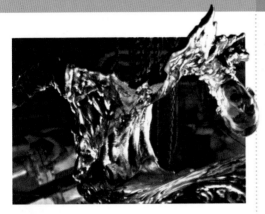

In Terminator 2: Judgment Day, *the character T-1000 was able to twist into any shape.*

TERMINATOR 2: JUDGMENT DAY

Just two years after *The Abyss*, James Cameron returned with another computer graphics milestone. *Terminator 2: Judgment Day*, the sequel to 1984's *The Terminator*, tells the story of an android from the future that travels back in time to the present to protect a boy who will one day save the world. The movie's villain is an android that is made of liquid metal and can change into any shape.

Once again, Cameron teamed up with ILM to provide the jaw-dropping special effects. Computer graphics brought the character to life, allowing it to melt, walk through walls, and change its face. *Terminator 2* was also one of the first movies to use motion capture to animate computer-generated characters. Motion capture records the movements of actual actors and uses them to animate computer-generated characters. This practice would soon become a common tool for computer animators.

JURASSIC PARK

In Steven Spielberg's 1993 hit *Jurassic Park*, based on a best-selling novel by Michael Crichton, a billionaire brings extinct dinosaurs back to life to create a theme park. Spielberg originally planned to bring the dinosaurs to life by using a type of **stop-motion animation**, but ILM's Dennis Muren used test animations to convince him that the team could create realistic dinosaurs using computer graphics. Spielberg was impressed, and Muren's team used computer graphics to create many of the movie's most famous scenes.

TITANIC

History and fiction met in James Cameron's 1997 blockbuster *Titanic*. The movie tells the story of two fictional characters who fall in love aboard the *Titanic*, a real-life ship that hit an iceberg and sank in 1912. Cameron used state-of-the-art computer graphics to animate special effects as the ship crashed into the iceberg, split in half, and sank to the bottom of the ocean. These incredible effects helped *Titanic* become the most successful movie ever when it was released.

Titanic *broke box office records upon its release in 1997.*

Tablet computers and other portable devices put advanced computer graphics in the palm of your hand.

CHAPTER TWO

TODAY'S GREATEST GRAPHICS

Computer graphics technology changes fast. Modern graphics are a far cry from the primitive lines and shapes produced by earlier equipment. Animators take advantage of the latest technology to create convincing human faces, lifelike textures, and water that looks real enough to drink. They can create hair that sways lightly in a breeze or clouds of dirt that fly up from the ground as a helicopter lands.

As graphics technology advances, it also becomes less expensive. This makes it available to more people. Today, millions of people all around the world see computer graphics every time they check the weather forecast, get a checkup at the doctor's office, or answer a cell phone call. As a result, graphics engineers now work in dozens of fields.

GRAPHICS IN GAMES

1962	1970s	1972	1996
Spacewar! helps popularize video games.	Flight simulators use computer graphics for the first time.	The Magnavox Odyssey becomes the first home video game console.	Mass production of 3D graphics chips for the Nintendo 64 console helps makes 3D graphics cheaper to produce.

VIDEO MONITORS PROVIDE REALISTIC GRAPHICS.

JOYSTICK CONTROLS SIMILAR TO THOSE USED FOR VIDEO GAME SYSTEMS

Many flight simulators use multiple video screens to reproduce the full visual range pilots have when they are in the air.

SIMULATING REALITY

Graphics-driven **simulations** have become powerful teaching tools. Simulations allow trainees to learn complex skills without the risks involved with actually engaging in a dangerous activity. For example, aircraft pilots climb into flight simulators as a part of their training. These simulators look like real airplane cockpits, but instead of windows they have video screens that show computer-generated worlds. The pilots can learn to fly without fear of crashing or damaging a real aircraft.

Simulations have also taken on a large role in military training. Combat simulators provide training without the use of expensive ammunition or risk of injury. The U.S. Army's Engagement Skills Trainer is similar to a video game. It can simulate many kinds of firearms, combat environments, weather, and other situations.

Medical schools use simulators to train healthcare professionals. Physicians use computer graphics technology to learn complex surgical procedures and study the inner workings of the human body.

SCIENTIFIC SOLUTIONS

Scientists have come to rely on computer graphics as a way to present their findings and study the work of other scientists. For example, they might use computer-generated charts, maps, or graphs to help illustrate important measurements in the articles and books they write.

Most people are familiar with the computer graphics used in **meteorology**. Weather stations and satellites take measurements and feed the information into computer systems. Meteorologists use information-rich graphics provided by these computers in making their forecasts. They also use computers to create easy-to-understand graphics showing storm movements and other weather patterns. These graphics are broadcast on television and posted online for people to get an idea about upcoming weather.

Computers represent weather patterns using animated, colored graphics.

COLORED GRAPHICS SHOW HOW POWERFUL DIFFERENT PARTS OF A STORM ARE.

GETTING REAL

Today's home video game consoles are capable of producing detailed, high-resolution 3D graphics that can look almost real. While the spaceships in *Spacewar!* were drawn using just a few lines, a single spaceship in a modern video game might be rendered from millions of **polygons**. Detailed textures and lighting systems help the model look even more realistic.

Creating computer graphics at this level of detail requires a lot of manpower. For example, an entire team of graphic artists and engineers might work on creating the lighting and shadows for a single game. As the technology that powers game systems continues to improve, graphics will continue to become more realistic. Soon, you might have trouble telling the difference between a video game and a live-action movie!

The realistic graphics in video games for modern consoles such as the Xbox 360 can take millions of dollars and several years to produce.

The popular Ice Age *series includes four feature-length films, several shorts, and a television special.*

ANIMATION REVOLUTION

In 1995, Pixar proved with *Toy Story* that computer-animated movies could compete with traditional hand-drawn animation. Since then, computer animation has become incredibly popular, and other companies have formed to challenge Pixar. DreamWorks Animation, co-founded by Steven Spielberg, entered the field with 1998's *Antz*. *Antz* competed head-to-head with Pixar's *A Bug's Life* and was able to hold its own both critically and commercially. DreamWorks continued to produce popular computer-animated movies, including the *Shrek* and *Kung Fu Panda* series. In 2002, *Ice Age* put Blue Sky Studios on the map as the next big thing in computer animation. Like Pixar, it developed its own software system. The software, called CGI Studio, uses a powerful but very expensive technique called ray tracing to render graphics. Blue Sky has used it to create such popular films as *Rio* and *Robots*.

CHRIS WEDGE

Animator Chris Wedge is one of the founders of Blue Sky Studios. Wedge co-directed the company's first two hits, *Ice Age* and *Robots*. He also directed the 2013 fantasy adventure *Epic*. In addition to his work behind the scenes, Wedge provides the voice of Scrat in the *Ice Age* series.

FROM THIS TO THAT

Actors John Goodman and Billy Crystal provided the voices of the main characters in Monsters, Inc.

Toy Story 3 *has been Pixar's biggest success so far at the box office.*

THE POWER OF PIXAR

After the release of early short films such as John Lasseter's *Luxo Jr.*, Pixar's computer-driven approach to animation took Hollywood by storm. Since then, the company has released a long string of blockbuster films, many of them among the most successful movies ever created. Pixar's success comes from its amazing skill at matching state-of-the-art computer graphics with memorable characters and engrossing stories. For each of its films, Pixar works to push the quality of its computer graphics farther and farther. Looking back at the company's movies provides an excellent view of the ways computer graphics have improved over the years.

THE MINDS BEHIND THE MOVIES

John Lasseter was the first creator to help make a name for Pixar, both with his early short films and his direction of the first three full-length Pixar films. While Lasseter continues to direct Pixar movies, many other creators have also played a major role in Pixar's success. After helping create the stories for the first two *Toy Story* movies, Pete Docter went on to direct *Monsters, Inc.* and *Up.* Andrew Stanton helped write Pixar's first four films before directing 2003's *Finding Nemo* and 2008's *WALL-E.* Though these creators are among the most famous people at Pixar, each film is actually the result of teamwork among dozens of people, from writers and animators to sound designers and voice actors. Making a computer-animated movie is a lot of work!

Finding Nemo *featured the voices of Albert Brooks as Marlin (bottom) and Ellen DeGeneres as Dory (top).*

REAPING THE REWARDS

Every one of Pixar's films has been a major hit at the box office. Even its least successful films have sold hundreds of millions of dollars in theater tickets, while its biggest smash, *Toy Story 3*, drew in over a billion dollars. Merchandise based on the films and home video sales are also major moneymakers.

Pixar's films are more than just moneymakers, though. They have also received praise from critics and audiences alike for their strong storylines, sharp humor, and unforgettable characters. As a result, the films have been nominated for hundreds of major awards in categories ranging from writing and directing to animation and special effects. ✳

1995
Toy Story

1998
A Bug's Life

1999
Toy Story 2

2001
Monsters, Inc.

2003
Finding Nemo

2004
The Incredibles

2006
Cars

2007
Ratatouille

2008
WALL-E

2009
Up

2010
Toy Story 3

2011
Cars 2

2012
Brave

2013
Monsters University

MASSIVE allowed filmmakers to fill battle scenes in the Lord of the Rings *movies with thousands of soldiers, each one displaying unique behavior.*

MASSIVE Moments

In the past, moviemakers shooting a big battle scene had to hire hundreds of people called extras to act as an army. Each one of these people had to be costumed and paid, making the process very expensive. As a result, many filmmakers were forced to scale down their plans for large battle scenes for budget reasons.

This problem was solved thanks to advances in computer graphics technology. Stephen Regelous's MASSIVE (Multiple Agent Simulation System in Virtual Environment) software was first put to use in creating the vast armies in the *Lord of the Rings* movies. MASSIVE can render millions of individual "agents" at once. Each agent relies on an artificial intelligence code that tells it how to behave. Animators can program the agents to fight each other, socialize, cheer for sports teams, or anything else they can think of. MASSIVE has been used in many films, including *300*, *Avatar*, and *WALL-E*.

MATCHING THE MOTIONS

The huge battle scenes powered by MASSIVE weren't the only way the *Lord of the Rings* movies wowed audiences with computer graphics. They also featured a computer-generated character named Gollum whose realistic movements helped him blend in perfectly with the real-life actors.

Gollum's lifelike motions were created using a process called motion capture. Actor Andy Serkis performed Gollum's scenes alongside the other actors while wearing a special suit with sensors attached. Computers used the sensors to record Serkis's movements, and animators attached those movements to the computer-generated Gollum model. As a result, the character moved exactly as Serkis had in each scene. Similar technology was used to create the character of Jar Jar Binks in *Star Wars Episode I: The Phantom Menace*, and actor Tom Hanks wore a motion capture suit to portray several characters in *The Polar Express*. Motion capture is also used often to create realistic movements for the characters in video games.

The Polar Express *earned a place in* Guinness World Records *as the first movie to be filmed entirely using motion capture technology.*

MODERN MARVEL

Avatar *director James Cameron (seated) worked with a cast that included Sam Worthington (right) and Joel David Moore (left).*

Human actors provided the realistic facial movements of the Na'vi alien characters in Avatar.

JAMES CAMERON'S *AVATAR*

No film has taken computer graphics technology farther than James Cameron's 2009 blockbuster *Avatar*. This time, Cameron teamed with the visual effects company Weta Digital, best known for its work on the *Lord of the Rings* series. Cameron, as in his past films, asked for computer-generated effects so advanced that engineers, animators, and programmers had to invent a variety of new and improved technology to make the movie happen. In fact, Cameron originally planned to begin filming *Avatar* in 1997, but he was forced to wait when he discovered that it would not be possible to make the movie the way he wanted using the technology available at the time.

FACE-TO-FACE

Weta had broken new ground in realistic facial animations with Gollum in the *Lord of the Rings* movies. Cameron asked the company to update its facial capture technology to make the faces of *Avatar's* Na'vi aliens even more lifelike than Gollum's.

Weta's technicians built a cap that fit onto an actor's head. A camera attached to the cap arced in front of the actor's face to record close-up video footage of the face in motion. The cap, meanwhile, recorded the movements of the actor's facial muscles. Animators then used all of the information to give the computer-generated Na'vi faces the kind of realism never seen before in movies. The Na'vi models could display even the actors' smallest, most subtle facial movements. This enabled them to express complex emotions.

Avatar also pioneered new technology for allowing actors to interact with computer-generated characters. Before *Avatar*, human actors in computer-generated scenes had to act in front of blank screens. The visual effects team dropped computer-generated characters and backgrounds onto the screen space later. Because they could not actually see the computer-generated characters or environments as they performed, the actors had to use their imaginations.

Avatar's specially built camera rig let Cameron see the computer graphics at the same time as the actors did their work. This system allowed Cameron to help the actors interact with the computer-generated Na'vi and their surroundings, enabling them to give more realistic performances.

AN IMMERSIVE EXPERIENCE

Cameron wanted the *Avatar* theatrical experience to draw audiences into the film's world unlike any movie had ever done before. The movie was designed to take advantage of the latest theater technology, including high definition 3D projectors and gigantic IMAX screens. ✳

It cost more than $300 million to bring the amazing world of Avatar *to the big screen.*

At Pixar, dozens of animators worked together as part of the team that created Toy Story 3.

3

ON THE JOB

E ven when animators and artists have the latest technology at their fingertips, creating modern computer graphics can still be an incredibly difficult, time-consuming process. Whether they are making an animated film, a video game, or special effects for a live-action movie, the members of a computer graphics team push themselves and their co-workers to do the best work they can.

Early examples of computer graphics were often created by single artists working alone at their computers. Because computers were not powerful enough to render detailed images, the artists could create simple graphics quickly and easily. Today, however, it would be impossible for a single animator to create all of the graphics for a movie or a video game. Instead, large teams work together to create detailed, realistic computer graphics. Within these teams, different workers specialize in different parts of the process.

FOUNDING THE FUTURE

1975	1982	1986	1993
George Lucas founds the visual effects company Industrial Light & Magic.	Adobe Systems is founded by Charles Geschke and John Warnock.	Steve Jobs purchases Lucasfilm's Graphics Group and turns it into Pixar.	Weta Digital is founded by Peter Jackson, Richard Taylor, and Jamie Selkirk.

Modelers use cutting-edge computer software to build the characters and objects that populate the world of a movie or video game.

SCULPTING NEW WORLDS

A 3D modeler uses computer software to build the 3D objects that make up a computer-generated scene, from characters and vehicles to landscapes and buildings. These 3D models are built using polygons. A single character model in a modern film or video game might be made up of millions of individual polygons.

Modelers use a variety of techniques to build their creations. Box modeling is a simple way for a modeler to quickly create a rough, blocky sketch of a model's overall shape. Spline modeling, also known as patch modeling or parametric surface modeling, allows a modeler to create the curved shapes needed for human or animal models. 3D modelers need to know how to use such software as 3ds Max or Maya. Math skills are also an important part of the job.

MODELS IN MOTION

3D animators bring computer graphics to life by using software to make 3D models move. They create everything from character movements and huge explosions to small background details such as a flag waving in the breeze. Animators might specialize in certain tasks. For example, one member of an animation team might specialize in facial movements while another focuses on explosions and other special effects.

Some animations are created from scratch. The animators use powerful software to program how each point of a 3D model will move, how fast it will go, and how smooth its path will be. Other times, animators rely on math and physics to ensure that objects move as they would in reality. For example, they might make use of a program that simulates the way hair or cloth moves in the wind. Animators might also use motion capture techniques. Motion capture often results in more realistic animations.

Devices attached to a motion capture suit record the movements of different body parts and map them to points on a 3D model.

THE ARTISTIC SIDE

Artwork for The Incredibles *provided animators with ideas for how the movie's characters should move.*

FROM CONCEPT TO COMPLETION

Though computer graphics are rooted in math and technology, art also plays a major role in their creation. One of the most important artistic positions on a computer graphics team is that of the concept artist. A concept artist is responsible for creating drawings, paintings, sculptures, and other artwork that provide an idea of what the final product should look like. The rest of the team uses the concept art as a guide as they design and build the 3D computer graphics.

SKETCHING IT OUT

This artwork from Pixar's 2004 computer animated hit *The Incredibles* shows Bob, one of the movie's heroes. In the lower-right corner, we can see an idea of what Bob's face will look like in the finished movie. Along the top of the page, we can see an idea for what kind of movements Bob would make if he jumped through the air.

FROM THE PAGE TO THE SCREEN

The image below shows a finished scene from *The Incredibles*. Notice Bob's similarities to the early sketch of the character. Facial features such as his huge jaw have been carried over to the final product as the computer-generated character was created from the hand-drawn sketch. ☀

Actor Craig T. Nelson provided the voice of Bob.

"[*The Incredibles* is] another example of Pixar's mastery of popular animation." —Film critic Roger Ebert

SKIN-DEEP

A completed 3D model looks like a colorless shape. It is like a clay sculpture that has yet to be painted. Texture artists are the members of animation teams who "paint" 3D models. They create colorful, textured skins for everything from trees and rocks to faces and clothing. Texture artists combine their artistic abilities and computer skills to create these details. They carefully examine real-life examples of wood, metal, skin, and other surfaces. They also have an in-depth understanding of how different colors and shades work together to present different effects to the viewer. Software such as Photoshop and 3ds Max helps them finalize their creations.

Textures can turn a colorless 3D shape into a realistic creature, such as this cave troll from The Lord of the Rings.

As the lead effects artist on Shrek the Third, *Matt Baer helped make sure the movie's lighting looked realistic.*

SUNSHINE AND SHADOWS

Lighting is a big part of making realistic computer graphics. Without effects such as shadows and reflections, computer graphics often look flat and cartoonish, no matter how good the models and textures are. At the same time, unrealistic lighting effects can be distracting and confusing to viewers. Lighting artists are responsible for avoiding these issues. They carefully analyze each scene to determine where light sources should be placed and how bright they should be. They also determine the color of the light. For example, the light from a flame might be yellow or orange, while the light from a fluorescent bulb might be bright white with shades of blue. Lighting artists also determine how the surfaces of models will absorb or reflect light. This creates effects such as streetlights reflected in puddles, moonlight gently shining through clouds, and glowing animal eyes.

AN INTERVIEW WITH DIGITAL ARTIST DIANA SEAR

Diana Sear is a digital lighting artist at Digital Domain, a company that has created digital artistry for blockbuster movies such as G.I. Joe, *the* Transformers *series,* The Day After Tomorrow, *and many more.*

When did you start thinking you wanted to work with computer graphics? Did any person or event inspire that career choice? I went to college at Savannah College of Art and Design (SCAD) in Georgia. SCAD requires all students to take a computer arts class. Somehow, I ended up in an advanced computer graphics class. I had never really worked with computer graphics before, but I liked it a lot. I ended up switching my major to computer art.

What kinds of classes should a would-be computer graphics artist look to take in middle school, high school, and beyond? Math classes are important for anyone who works in digital effects. Algebra, geometry, and **trigonometry** are all important. Physics classes are also important, especially for people who are working on digital explosions.

A person has to work her way up to being a computer graphics artist. What other projects and jobs did you do in school and your work life before the opportunity to create digital effects for movies came along? How did that work prepare you? In college, I did a lot of group projects. It helped me learn how to work with people from different backgrounds and prepared me for the kind of collaboration my job requires today. I also attended SIGGRAPH

(Special Interest Group on GRAPHics and Interactive Techniques) conferences in college. There, I got to trade ideas with other artists, show off my work, and meet people in the industry.

It takes an entire team to design and build state-of-the-art computer graphics. Does working as part of a team come naturally to you, or was it something you had to learn and work on? Working as part of a group was pretty natural to me, but you can always work to improve your communication skills. You have to learn to adapt to working with many different kinds of people who have different backgrounds and different ways of thinking.

Do you have a particular project that you're especially proud of, or that you think really took your work to another level? How did you feel going into it and during the process? The most rewarding thing I worked on was the movie *Transformers: Dark of the Moon*. I was the lighting lead for the character Laserbeak, an evil bird robot assassin. The reason the project was so rewarding was that I got to work on it from the very beginning and see it all the way through to the end. On some projects, you might only work on something for a few weeks before moving on to something else. With *Transformers*, I helped design the character's look by working with

other artists to select colors, shading, and textures. I followed Laserbeak's entire process, from the earliest stages to working with compositors to place him in the finished movie.

Let's say someone gave you whatever you needed to build your dream project. What would it be? If I had all the time and money I needed, I would probably want to create a music video with really incredible visual effects. Unfortunately, I don't have enough time!

What advice would you give to a young person who wants to create computer-generated art for movies? It's important to understand the entire process of creating computer graphics and know how something goes from an idea to a finished project. However, the best way to get a job is to specialize in one part of the process, such as lighting, modeling, or animation. It's much easier to find a job if you are really good at one thing instead of only being sort of good at everything. ✳

Diana Sear helped create the digital effects for Transformers: Dark of the Moon.

UNDER THE HOOD

Modelers, animators, and artists all rely on powerful software to help them do their jobs. But the technology they have isn't always able to do everything they need it to do. Graphics software engineers solve these problems by investigating new ways to render digital images. They work with other team members to figure out what a project needs. If the software to complete a certain task does not exist, an engineer may write computer code for a new program. He or she then helps designers and artists learn how to use the new techniques. A typical graphics software engineer knows computer-programming languages such as C++. Engineers also have highly developed math skills. Because they work with graphics, they tend to have some background in art. This helps them understand the needs of modelers, animators, and artists.

Programmers put in long hours writing the code that powers computer graphics software.

In movies such as Tron: Legacy, *which blends live-action performances with computer-animated environments, compositors must make the final product look convincingly realistic.*

ALL TOGETHER NOW

Compositors are team members who tie together animation, special effects, live-action footage, backgrounds, and the other elements that make up a computer-generated scene. They are responsible for making sure that each element blends together smoothly and maintains a certain style. This ensures that none of the individual effects stand out to audiences as something that doesn't belong.

Compositors occupy an important leadership role. If a compositor notices that more work is needed on a certain element of a scene, he or she guides the artists and designers involved to make sure they get it exactly right. At the same time, he or she works with other team leaders to keep the project moving forward. Compositors must be able to communicate well, juggle many jobs, pay attention to details, and make big decisions. Because of this, it takes years of experience and success to land a job as a compositor.

The computer-generated Gollum character in the Lord of the Rings trilogy helped all three films win Academy Awards for visual effects.

4

FROM IDEA TO IMAGE

E ven with a large team of artists, animators, and engineers working their hardest, it can take years to bring a big budget movie or video game from an idea to a finished product. Though it might last only a split second, a single computer graphics shot in a movie could be the product of countless work hours and thousands of dollars. Because every project is such a major investment of time and money, team members are always under pressure to make sure they deliver high quality results.

Such effort makes sense. Audiences have a history of rejecting bad computer graphics. No matter how good the rest of a movie or a video game is, poor graphics or effects can ruin its chances of success. Getting the graphics right is a must for the entertainment companies that put millions of dollars on the line.

MOVIE MAGIC

1982	1991	2001	2009
Tron *becomes one of the first movies to feature computer-generated animation.*	Terminator 2: Judgment Day *breaks new ground with its computer-generated villain.*	MASSIVE *software generates huge armies for* The Lord of the Rings: The Fellowship of the Ring.	Avatar *makes use of breakthrough facial capture software.*

LAYING THE GROUNDWORK

The process of creating computer graphics begins with an idea. For example, take an important computer-generated character like Gollum in the *Lord of the Rings* series. Long before filming began, artists and animators brainstormed the character's look with the films' director, Peter Jackson. Because the films were based on a series of books, Jackson and his team already had a general description of what Gollum should look like. However, they also had their own ideas about how the character should be portrayed on the screen. Together, they worked with concept artists to explore as many ideas as possible. Eventually, they settled on a design similar to the one seen in the finished movies.

Artwork from a 1978 animated version of the Lord of the Rings *stories inspired the animators working on the live-action movies.*

Lord of the Rings *director Peter Jackson began making movies when he was just eight years old.*

EXPLORING THE POSSIBILITIES

Because computer graphics are dependent not just on imagination but also upon budgets and available technology, creators must consider whether the designs they want to use are both possible and within the limits of their project.

After getting a general idea about a character's design, animators offer their opinions about what current animation software can and cannot do with the character. If necessary, they might begin working with engineers and programmers to plan new software or other technological solutions. Gollum was a huge leap forward for the use of computer graphics in live-action movies. As an important character in the films, he would be required to interact with the other actors for long scenes. The team had to come up with new technology that allowed Gollum to blend seamlessly with human actors.

Joe Letteri was one of many computer graphics artists who worked on the Lord of the Rings *movies.*

FROM THE PAGE TO THE SCREEN

Once the team had settled on a final design for Gollum and had begun creating the technology necessary to bring him to life, the creature had to make the leap from an idea to a 3D computer model. Artists began the process by creating a life-size sculpture of the character. The special effects team at Weta Digital, the company handling the movies' visual effects, then scanned the sculpture with a laser to create a 3D digital Gollum model.

Texture artists then digitally painted skin, clothes, and other features onto the digital model. Typically, computer-generated skin and clothes look better from a distance. As the view closes in, the animation tends to look less realistic. Part of the reason is that real-life cloth and skin are complicated surfaces. Even the most powerful technology available limits animators from matching the immense complexity of either.

THE DEVIL'S IN THE DETAILS

When a computer-generated character model comes close to looking real, small imperfections create an effect known as the uncanny valley. Instead of being drawn into the film, audiences are distracted and sometimes unsettled by the characters. Lifeless eyes are an especially difficult problem for animators to solve.

Films such as *The Polar Express* and *The Curious Case of Benjamin Button* both used state-of-the-art methods to create realistic computer-generated human characters. Though both films were successful, critics and audiences alike noted that the characters never looked entirely human.

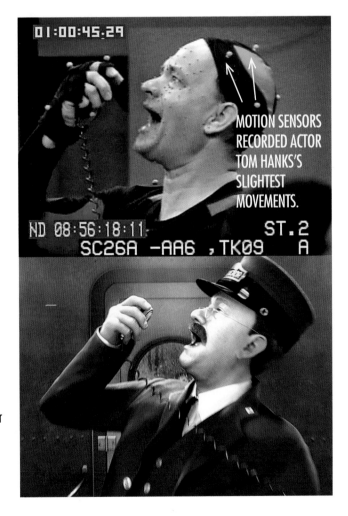

MOTION SENSORS RECORDED ACTOR TOM HANKS'S SLIGHTEST MOVEMENTS.

Even though actor Tom Hanks wore the latest in motion capture technology for his performance in The Polar Express, *some viewers found the computer-animated characters unrealistic.*

WHERE THE MAGIC HAPPENS

Weta Digital founders Peter Jackson (second from right) and Jamie Selkirk (right) have worked with movie legends such as Robert Zemeckis (left) and Michael J. Fox (second from left).

WETA DIGITAL

Weta Digital is a visual effects company that was founded in 1993 in New Zealand by director Peter Jackson and two of his longtime associates, Richard Taylor and Jamie Selkirk. Weta Digital's team works with animation, modeling, and motion capture technology. A sister company, Weta Workshop, makes props, costumes, and models for movies.

Weta became world famous for its groundbreaking work on Jackson's *Lord of the Rings* movies. Since then, the company has been in high demand among filmmakers, and their work has been featured in many Hollywood blockbusters.

PETER JACKSON

Peter Jackson has shown a love for special effects since the very beginning of his career as a filmmaker. His first full-length film was 1987's *Bad Taste*, a low-budget, comedic horror story. Though they did not have a lot of money to work with, Jackson and his team drew attention for the movie's clever special effects. Other early films, such as *Dead Alive*, followed a similar path and helped increase Jackson's reputation as a master of creative effects. He began drawing interest from major movie studios. As his budgets grew larger, Jackson began incorporating advanced computer graphics into his films.

THE FRIGHTENERS

One of Weta's earliest triumphs was Jackson's 1996 film *The Frighteners*. The movie tells the story of a man who can see and communicate with ghosts. Like many of Jackson's earlier films, it is a blend of comedy and horror. Though the film received mixed reviews and was not a financial success, its special effects were widely praised. The team at Weta used a combination of makeup and computer animation to create the film's ghost characters.

Critics praised the incredible visual effects of The Frighteners.

BACK TO MIDDLE-EARTH

After the success of the *Lord of the Rings* trilogy, Peter Jackson announced that he would bring *The Hobbit* to the big screen as a series of three films. *The Hobbit* is set in the same world as *The Lord of the Rings* and features many of the same characters, including Gollum, but takes place in an earlier time. Once again, Gollum's appearance and movements were based on the performance of actor Andy Serkis. However, thanks to the improvements in animation technology since the *Lord of the Rings* films were created, animators at Weta were able to make the character more detailed and convincing than ever before. ✳

Gollum wowed audiences with his realistic computer-generated facial expressions.

FACING OFF

A nonhuman character such as Gollum gives creators a little more room for imperfection because audiences do not have previous ideas about what he should look like. However, the team at Weta still had to tweak the details to make sure he looked like a creature who could realistically exist alongside humans.

Faces present some of the biggest challenges in designing a computer-generated character. To make sure Gollum did not fall into the uncanny valley, the animation team built a program that utilized dozens of sliding control bars to operate the face's lips, nostrils, wrinkles, and other features. Some sliders even control the movements of tiny hairs. Andy Serkis wore motion capture sensors on his face to help guide the animators.

A MONSTER'S MOVEMENTS

The next step was to make sure Gollum's movements looked just as believable as his character model. The team wanted to make sure that his motions seemed natural. To accomplish this, they used a combination of motion capture and manual animation.

For scenes in which Gollum was simply walking or talking to other characters, the animators applied Andy Serkis's movements to the Gollum model. They then tweaked the movements and added small details such as finger and facial movements. They even designed a system that animated the small movements Gollum's body would make when breathing.

For some scenes, Gollum needed to perform movements that a human could not. For example, he is shown climbing up and down flat cliff surfaces like a lizard or an insect. Animators created these movements from scratch, as a human actor could not climb in such a way.

Andy Serkis won many awards for his portrayal of Gollum.

LASTING CONTRIBUTIONS

Ray Harryhausen poses with some of the models for the 1981 film Clash of the Titans.

STOP AND GO

Stop-motion animation is a process in which an animator photographs a physical object such as a model or doll, moves the physical object a tiny amount, and shoots it again. Each photograph becomes a single frame of animation.

Though very time-consuming, the process grew in popularity because it allowed animators to use 3D objects and environments instead of flat drawings. With the rise of computer graphics in the 1990s and 2000s, stop-motion animation became less and less common in films. However, it has become popular again in recent years because of its unique visual style.

In 2005, Peter Jackson directed a retelling of *King Kong* that used computer graphics to animate the gorilla.

THE EARLY DAYS

Stop-motion animation dates to the earliest days of film. The first examples appeared in the late 1800s, and it continued to be a popular animation style throughout the early 1900s. One of the most respected stop-motion animators of this era was Willis O'Brien. O'Brien created stop-motion dinosaurs for 1925's *The Lost World* and the famous giant gorilla of 1933's *King Kong*. In the 1940s, Ray Harryhausen began a successful career in stop-motion. He animated sea monsters, flying saucers, and the famous skeleton warriors in 1963's *Jason and the Argonauts*.

REACHING A PEAK

Though the technology involved did not change much, stop-motion animation was often used to create special effects in the following decades. In the 1980s, computer graphics pioneers such as George Lucas,

The AT-AT walkers of The Empire Strikes Back *were created using stop-motion animation.*

Steven Spielberg, and James Cameron put it to use in their early films. The AT-AT walkers in Lucas's *The Empire Strikes Back* were created using stop-motion, as was the killer robot in Cameron's first *Terminator* movie. However, these same creators, along with others, gradually began to replace the technique with computer animation.

Computer graphics offered a more realistic look while taking less time and effort to create. Within a few years, stop-motion animation had become a rarity in films.

BACK IN ACTION

Some filmmakers eventually came to appreciate the art of stop-motion animation. Director Henry Selick kicked off a long run of successful stop-motion films with 1993's *The Nightmare Before Christmas*. Selick's 2009 film *Coraline* combined traditional stop-motion animation with advanced 3D filming techniques. The same year, director Wes Anderson scored a hit by bringing Roald Dahl's classic novel *Fantastic Mr. Fox* to the big screen as a stop-motion animated movie. After more than a hundred years, this unique animation style is still going strong. ✺

Coraline *was based on a book by author Neil Gaiman.*

Thanks to the team's hard work, Gollum was able to blend in seamlessly with real actors such as Sean Astin.

FINISHING TOUCHES

Before Gollum was inserted into the film, the footage showed Andy Serkis in his motion capture body suit interacting with the actors. Because Serkis is larger than the Gollum model, the team could not simply swap the Gollum model into the place where Serkis once stood. The animators began the process by creating what they called reference shots. They digitally removed Serkis from the film and replaced him with the animated Gollum model. To make up for the size difference between Serkis and Gollum, they often copied part of the background and pasted it over the space where Serkis had stood. Other times, they created dust clouds and other effects to fill the space.

The filmmakers and actors used this reference footage to film the scenes a second time. This time, Serkis stayed offscreen and read his lines aloud while the other actors recreated their performances. This gave the filmmakers clean footage into which they could insert the animated Gollum model.

YESTERDAY, TODAY, AND TOMORROW

The first *Lord of the Rings* film premiered in 2001 to rave reviews and major box office success. Though almost every aspect of the movie met with praise, the computer animation, and especially Gollum, attracted the most attention.

At the time the film was released, its computer graphics were at the cutting edge of technology. Audiences were blown away by Weta Digital's accomplishments. But while the animation still looks good today, more recent films, such as *Avatar*, have surpassed it. This is the way technology works. Just as the computer graphics in *Space Invaders* or *Tron* seem out of date and unrealistic now, films and video games of the future will surpass the efforts of today's greatest animators.

Will you be among the artists, animators, and engineers who help move computer graphics forward?

Gollum returned to the big screen in 2012 in The Hobbit: An Unexpected Journey, *the first part of a* Lord of the Rings *prequel trilogy.*

THE FUTURE

Sony announced its plans for the PlayStation 4 in February 2013.

EXPLORING NEW WORLDS

Computer technology is constantly improving and evolving, and filmmakers and video game companies do their best to stay on the cutting edge. Many of the same creators who pushed the medium forward in its earlier days are still making major innovations. James Cameron, Steven Spielberg, and Peter Jackson continue to blur the lines between animation and reality with their films, and the animators at Pixar, DreamWorks, and other companies are creating imaginative worlds that are carefully designed down to the smallest detail. As time goes on, a new generation of filmmakers and animators will push the limits of computer graphics even farther. At the same time, new video game consoles such as Sony's PlayStation 4 will offer developers the power to create photorealistic virtual worlds.

CHANGING TECHNOLOGY

When it comes to creating amazing computer graphics, the talented artists and storytellers who create them are limited only by the power of today's latest technology. More powerful computers and improved technology for displaying video will open up more possibilities for creators to design the next big thing in computer graphics.

The rise in popularity of 3D TVs has brought eye-popping 3D images to living rooms around the world, and technology companies are experimenting with wearable headsets that can fully immerse video game players by surrounding their entire field of vision with advanced computer graphics. A true virtual reality experience powered by computer graphics might not be far off!

3D movies have become a popular form of home entertainment.

CAREER STATS

MULTIMEDIA ARTISTS AND ANIMATORS

MEDIAN ANNUAL SALARY (2010): $58,510

NUMBER OF JOBS (2010): 66,500

PROJECTED JOB GROWTH: 8%, slower than average

PROJECTED INCREASE IN JOBS 2010–2020: 5,500

REQUIRED EDUCATION: Bachelor's degree in art, computer graphics, computer programming, or a related field

LICENSE/CERTIFICATION: Certification may be necessary for certain jobs

SOFTWARE DEVELOPERS

MEDIAN ANNUAL SALARY (2010): $90,530

NUMBER OF JOBS (2010): 913,100

PROJECTED JOB GROWTH: 30%, much faster than average

PROJECTED INCREASE IN JOBS 2010–2020: 270,900

REQUIRED EDUCATION: Bachelor's degree in computer science plus programming skills and experience

LICENSE/CERTIFICATION: Certification may be necessary for certain jobs

COMPUTER PROGRAMMERS

MEDIAN ANNUAL SALARY (2010): $71,380

NUMBER OF JOBS (2010): 363,100

PROJECTED JOB GROWTH: 12%, average

PROJECTED INCREASE IN JOBS 2010–2020: 43,700

REQUIRED EDUCATION: Bachelor's degree required for most jobs, but some positions require only an associate's degree

LICENSE/CERTIFICATION: Certification may provide an advantage when competing for jobs but is not generally required

Figures reported by the United States Bureau of Labor Statistics

RESOURCES

BOOKS

Cohn, Jessica. *Animator*. Pleasantville, NY: Gareth Stevens, 2010.

Egan, Jill. *How Video Game Designers Use Math*. New York: Chelsea House, 2009.

Mullins, Matt. *Multimedia Artist and Animator*. Ann Arbor, MI: Cherry Lake, 2010.

Sande, Warren, and Carter Sande. *Hello World! Computer Programming for Kids and Other Beginners*. Greenwich, CT: Manning, 2009.

Svitil, Torene. *So You Want to Work in Animation and Special Effects?* Berkeley Heights, NJ: Enslow, 2008.

FACTS FOR NOW

Visit this Scholastic Web site
for more information on computer graphics:
www.factsfornow.scholastic.com
Enter the keywords **Computer Graphics**

GLOSSARY

icons (EYE-kahnz) graphic symbols on a computer screen representing programs, functions, or files

interfaces (IN-tur-fay-siz) the point at which two different things meet; for example, a keyboard is an interface between a computer and a user

meteorology (mee-tee-uh-RAH-luh-jee) the study of the atmosphere and weather

photorealistic (foh-toh-REE-uh-liss-tik) looking exactly like reality

polygons (PAH-li-gahnz) shapes with three or more sides; triangles, squares, pentagons, and hexagons are all polygons

render (REN-dur) to make or cause to become; a computer renders graphics based on the designs of artists

shading (SHAY-ding) making parts of an image darker by reproducing the effects of shade

simulations (sim-yuh-LAY-shuhnz) trial runs to act out real events

stop-motion animation (STAHP MOH-shuhn an-uh-MAY-shuhn) a process in which an animator photographs a physical object such as a model or doll, moves the physical object a tiny amount, and shoots it again to create frames of animation

textures (TEKS-churz) the outer layers of 3D models that show how they would feel, such as how rough or smooth they would be

trigonometry (trig-uh-NAH-muh-tree) the mathematical study of triangles

virtual (VUR-choo-uhl) made to seem like the real thing, but created using a computer

INDEX

Page numbers in *italics* indicate illustrations.

INDEX (CONTINUED)

ABOUT THE AUTHOR

KEVIN CUNNINGHAM graduated from the University of Illinois at Urbana. He is the author of more than 60 books on history, health, disasters, and other topics. He lives near Chicago, Illinois.